The National Poetry Series

D1515615

The National Poetry Series was established in 1978 to ensure the publication of five poetry books annually through five participating publishers. Publication is funded by the Lannan Foundation, Stephen Graham, the Joyce & Seward Johnson Foundation, Glenn & Renee Schaeffer, Juliet Lea Hillman Simonds, and the Edward T. Cone Foundation.

2010 Competition Winners

Lauren Berry of Houston, Texas, *The Lifting Dress*
Selected by Terrance Hayes, to be published by Penguin Books

William Billiter of Clinton, New York, *Stutter*
Selected by Hilda Raz, to be published by the University of Georgia Press

James Grinwis of Florence, Massachusetts, *Exhibit of Forking Paths*
Selected by Eleni Sikelianos, to be published by Coffee House Press

M. A. Vizsolyi of New York, New York, *The Lamp with Wings: Love Sonnets*
Selected by Ilya Kaminsky, to be published by HarperCollins Publishers

Laura Wetherington of Roanoke, Virginia, *A Map Predetermined and Chance*
Selected by C. S. Giscombe, to be published by Fence Books

Stutter

Stutter

POEMS BY WILLIAM BILLITER

The University of Georgia Press
Athens & London

Published by the University of Georgia Press
Athens, Georgia 30602
www.ugapress.org
© 2011 by William Billiter
All rights reserved
Designed by Walton Harris
Set in 10/15 Minion Pro
Printed and bound by Thomson-Shore

Printed in the United States of America

15   14   13   12   11   P   5   4   3   2   1

Library of Congress Cataloging-in-Publication Data

Billiter, William.
Stutter : poems / by William Billiter.
       p.   cm. — (The national poetry series)
ISBN-13: 978-0-8203-3881-1 (pbk. : alk. paper)
ISBN-10: 0-8203-3881-8 (pbk. : alk. paper)
I. Title.
PS3602.I447S78 2011
811'.6—dc22   2011004072

British Library Cataloging-in-Publication Data available

for Betsy, always

Contents

Acknowledgments

Grateful acknowledgement is made to the editors of these magazines in which the following poems, some in different form, originally appeared:

Atom Mind — "By Proxy" (originally titled "Walleye Lures")

Conduit — "Solitaire"

Northeast Corridor — "First Adultery"

Poetry East — "Depth Charge"

Stutter

After a Night of Steady Rain

Under these old   lindens a couple   of long ago
kids pressed   bare feet   into wet cement, left
imprints of their soles   in the sidewalk.   Water pools
in them now, little   baptismal fonts   in the lost church
of childhood. Go   ahead, no   one is looking. Kneel
down, dip   your fingers into those   sacred puddles,
anoint yourself   in the shade of the lindens.   The sap of all
saplings still   pulses through   crooked limbs.

Solitaire

Singular   trees   hold
fast   to these   fields.
A woman,   who   knows,
she   could be   the farmer's
wife,   turns   over
the ten   of spades,   lights
another   cigarette.   A tree
here,   a tree   there,
holding   fast.   They
say   it's best   to leave
them   alone,   plough
around   them,   they
keep   the earth   from slipping
away.   Soon   enough
the corn   will be   taller
than   any   man.
Roots   smoulder   in secret,
waiting   for rain.   The woman
drips   ash   onto
the table.   The tractor   raises
dust.   She   lights
another,   turns   over
the three   of hearts.   It's
impossible   to   cheat.

Migrations

When I was   a boy, I kept   things in a box —
broken skull of a skunk,   a buckeye,   a glass bead.
I kept the box   in the back of my   closet, buried
under shoes,   shells, shotguns,   an occasional
showgirl.   I was a bit of a   shut-in, unable
to shout down   the weather. But   once, I heard
the whole   note of a whooping   crane and wondered,
without want, if its   bones, too,   were hollow.

Acolytes at the Altar

Under the trestle,   them carps are big   as possums and bite
on doughballs. It's cane   poles and red pop   all afternoon.
Stink says they got   a mud vein like a catfish.   I don't
bother to check.   Stink says they's really   just giant goldfish,
same as you   win at the fair in them   little bowls of colored
water. They   just be bigger,   that's all, he says.
When his bobber   goes under, he   jerks the bamboo.
A train blares,   engine throttling down.   The sun strobes
between coalcars.   Dust spins under   the trestle a spell,
then all is   quiet again. Our   lines sag
in the slow brown   water, and the tin   scale stuck
on Stink's   face twinkles   and blinds.

Sweet Little Nothings

After the law left   and the dust in the lane
drifted into the sassafras   trees, Gethsemane
popped open her snuffbox,   cut a fresh
plug with her penknife,   spat at the cock
to make it shuck and jive.   A milksnake
curled in the rafters. The blue   tick twitched
under the porchswing. A barn   cat stretched.
Her husband's left   hand floated
free among   the blooming lily
pads, gold band   glinting. Gethsemane
gathered up her pitchfork,   the tines shined
like new dimes in the sun.   Oh she'd
be ready if they come   snooping again,
she'd sure enough   be ready.

At the Grain Elevator

Hauled ourselves up   the pulley lift, punched
the kill switch, found   him hunched over the corn
dryer, arm deep   in the stainless teeth of the augur.
Kernels stuck to the bone.   Blood muddied the dust.
Stink whipped off   his belt, twisted it taut,
a tourniquet above   the shredded elbow. Sirens.
Soup's face turned to paste.   He kept trying to jerk
that arm free. Two-ways   blared below. Somebody
shouted, Doc's here.   Corn dust swirled
sweet in our nostrils.   Hold him down now boys.
The bone saw slid   into place. Soup shucked us off,
gave one last tug   and was loose. His arm hung limp,
in strips, like raw bacon.   Stink said Christ Almighty, spit out
his chaw. Next harvest,   Soup was back. With a shift
of his shoulder, the steel claw   opened and closed like the mandibles
of a mantis. When the pinching started,   it felt just like a lit match
on bare skin. Sometimes   he'd latch onto Lloyd till he howled.
He'd let out a sort   of cackle then, and shift his shoulder,
that cold claw clicking   open and shut. We were all
helpless, each of us   with two good hands.

Snapshot from Shinbone

for Blanche Line

She kept her killing   axe in the pantry
with the canned peaches   and jars of pickled
pigs' feet. Spiders fed on   flies in the cornices.
Some kind of snake   the color of melon
slept in the sun   near the corncrib.
It was too dry for frogs,   ditches puckered
with weeds, dust in my mouth.   Grasshoppers spat
tobacco juice in the palms   of my hands. She
hung the sheets on a braided   line, washed
her hair under the hand   pump. When
the water finally come,   it sputtered out
the spout like new blood.   Too much iron
in this damned well,   she said, go now
and fetch us a chicken   from the yard,
grandson, it's getting on   supper time.

Covet

Twelve-gauge feels damned   heavy today.
I can't hit   a thing. Soup hollers
pull!, the clay   pigeons whir. He
empties both   barrels, smiles as the pieces
tumble into the muddy   field. I step up.
The shotgun kicks   at my heart, discs
spinning whole   into the woods. Soup sniggers,
draws a bead,   *crack! crack!* balls
of dust swirl   over the fence line. Another
smile. I bury   the stock in my shoulder, thinking
how he's got the most   prettiest wife in town.

Uncle Ersel's Thumbs

They was forked,   each pair
a divining rod   bent for Edna.
He could say   certain words,
even string   a few together
now and again,   but he never
did learn   to tie them
shoelaces.   What happened
was she'd been pretty   far along
with him when she   slipped in the pen
slopping the hogs.   They got
to her, the hogs   did. Hurt
her real bad.   She was made
to stay in bed   till it was her
time. When   Ersel finally
come, he had   them thumbs,
and a pig face.   That's the God's
honest truth.   He lived
a good long   time, short,
stooped, always   by Edna's side.
She bought him   a nice blonde
going to church   hat. Some
Sundays after   dinner, he'd
clean his nails   with a penknife
and try to whistle   along with the gospel
show on the radio.   He really
liked "Power   in the Blood." Oh
he really   did. Most
times, though,   he'd just sit
quiet there   by the stove
and twiddle all   them thumbs.

One for the Boy, Leaning

A dime's   in his pocket, a map's   on his wall, a red
dog's   by his side when he runs   down the road.
He   caught a crawdad   this morning, then
let   it go. Was that   the sun blinking
or just   a lost crow?   He's skipping
alone,   broken flag   in the rain. He's
been warned   not to go   back there,
back   of the knoll. Here   come the doctor
and preacher   again. His mother   pours coffee,
they   look out   on the pond. A hush
fills   the house like an echoing   fume. The boat's
moored   in the moonlight.   Fish flinch
in the shallows,   famished for flies.   He covers
his   face, light   and dark fuse.

Nothing Burns Quite So Good
As Your Daddy's Aftershave

Me and Stink   seined the Pusheeta,   frog gigs
tied to our wrists,   tin minnow   bucket submerged
near the bank.   We was after   water snakes.
A bullhead   slipped under   our net,
the snapper didn't.   We seen   no snakes
but we caught   a crawdad   bigger than Stink's
pecker, which ain't   saying much.   When nighthawks
flashed their starry   wings, we   cornered a possum
by the switchbox,   poked it with a bent   tent pole.
It didn't play   dead like they said.   It spit
and sputtered, broke   free and lit   after us
all the way   down the tracks   to Stink's house,
that old barber   shop his daddy   used to run
on the first floor   stockpiled with cases   of cut-rate
aftershave.   Stink knew   where he kept
the key. After   dark we drained   a dozen bottles,
struck Blue Tips,   two lines   of fire ripping
the trestle rails.   We stuffed   Black Cats
into the mouths   of the empties,   lit the wicks.
We run   like hellhounds   was on our heels.
Not fast   enough. Sweet   smelling glass
swarmed my legs   like yellow jackets.   Blood snaked
into my sneakers.   Stink didn't think   I needed
no stitches.   We caught   some crickets
for our snapper   and moseyed   on home.

Long about the Third Watch

Willy has the Black Cats   in his pockets, stink
bombs in his socks. I have   the matchbooks
and the bottle rockets, we   do slither
to the park. Soup spots   a cherry top
in the alley, breaks down   the river bank.
Me and Willy leap   the chain link,
duck behind a dumpster,   wait, wait.
Fuck it, says he, let's go   get us some hot
cross buns. We knock   the secret knock
on the bakery's back door.   It cracks
open leaking sugar   and grease and light.
Curfew's for punks, says he,   let's head
for the shack. We pass the sweet   bread, roll
a sticky j. Soup   don't never show.
Through the chinkhole, it   looks like someone
has pinched shut the soda pop   cap of the moon.

By Proxy

A boy is waving   from a boat   to a passing train.
A broken plough   rusts   in the sun. Menarche
of so many   lost   moments guiding
us back to this   place,   where sidewalks end
and the Johnny Appleseeds   bloom   again in the quicksilver
helix of our breathing.   Along   the tracks, silos
collapse, fences   collect   their dividends of debris.
Crows mob   a hawk   as the boy in the boat
tugs at the pond   he seems   stitched to like a patch
on a sleeve, arm   articulating   with a shoulder caught
in midcast,   the line   arcing out
over the water   where everything   is something, where we
all retreat   to weep   and panic and drown.

Where Are Our Dear Mothers

Soup slipped   on the stoop, split   open
his scalp. His chin   drooped, eyes   rolled
back like a rabbit's   when its neck   snares
quick in the run.   We peeled   back
his hair, skull   gleaming, a sliver   of moon.
Me and Stink   drove the back   roads.
Man, that   was some wild   ride.
Soup slumped   in the backseat,   white
lines bobbed   and weaved just   like Ali
doing the rope-   a-dope. Must've   been
the muscatel,   maybe   the horse
tranquilizers. We   got lost,   twice,
shook Soup   awake. Hospital   lights
buzzed like busy   signals. Soup   sent
a sloppy haymaker   over the doc's   head,
bawled, You   killed her, you   bastards, you
killed her.   C'mon man,   Stink says,
let him stitch   shut your stupid   head.
When his dad come,   he scooped   Soup
up and whispered,   Listen, son, they   tried
everything, listen,   they tried to   save her.

Pallbearers

I got dizzy   when the sirens come,
had to sit a spell. They   were bleeding pretty
badly. A finger twitched   in the ditch. A man
come along and put   it in a little
brown bag like it   was lunch or something.
They pulled a sheet   over the kid's
head. He wasn't   moving no
more. Sunlight   twinkled glass
in the road. It hurt   my eyes.
The kid's mother kept   on wailing
and bleeding. Somebody   shouted for something.
Wild canaries lit   on the barbed wire.
They didn't sing.   I tried
to think about nothing   and leaned back
in the dry weeds. A couple   ants tugged at
the corpse of a June bug,   drug it away.

Salt Lick

The dumb bastards   put blocks out,
built a tree   stand in the sugarbush,
shared a jug   to keep the chill off,
bowstrings   taut as tendons of the dead.
Does hooved   the powdered snow, stripped
bark from paper   birches. I've got nothing
against killing,   mind you, there being
a proper time   for all things. But
baiting deer   in the depths of winter is akin
to cheating at cards,   no telling what
men like that   will do, or not, depending
on who's   watching. The pretty one
twitches an ear,   breath floating like smoke.
Stink exhales,   flicks his fingers from the string,
swack. She   stumbles sideways, leaps
once, folds.   Let's haul her out,
says he.   I take another swig, nod.

While the Lips Cover the Teeth

Deadly Death sat on the dock   sipping a Dr. Pepper.
He was waiting for Willy, but Willy   wasn't nowhere
to be seen. Nope, he'd   split quick as a skink
startled from its sunning rock.   He'd reckoned that
raw rattle was meant for him   and made the mailtrain
to Mobile. Deadly Death dipped   his feet in the dark water,
leaned back on his elbows,   looked up at all
that blue sky. Some   kids played skipper
in a skiff, young bucks locked   in their little bone
lockers. It wasn't lust, but   loss he felt.
They'd have to wait their turn. Pity,   he thought, I
could so painlessly spare them   these paltry lives.

And They Were Scattered

The shepherds have come   with their see-through shields,
their nightsticks,   gas masks and goggles. But the sheep
have seen enough   of these shenanigans.
They brandish clubs,   spears rough hewn
from felled branches,   boards torn from barns.
They bare their broken   teeth and tether their hard
luck to the sketch   of the crucified one suspended
above them all.   The shepherds advance in lock
step toward   the flock, a line of silver
helmets flashing   under the cold sun.
The sheep are many.   Canisters of teargas hiss.
They circle one   another, the blows begin,
bloody bootprints   like dance steps painted on snow.
That angel abides   in the bleachers, broadsword drawn.

The Light Shall Not Be Clear nor Dark

The girl with the pouty   smile hangs
on her cross. She   says, See?
A child has drawn   stars and moons
on her right   hand, a sad
angel sits   on her left.
Muscled and   bare, she
has the torso   of a male dancer
twisting to a silent   beat, cobalt
blue veins   visible through black
tights. Someone   has stuck the tines
of a stainless fork   into her side.
Oil fires   rage in the desert
below, smoke   fouling the route
to the Red Sea.   And the cock
at her feet   does nothing
but stand   there, as if
it was a statue.   And the corpse
in the denim jacket   grins. It
has just told   the cock a dirty
joke. The girl   with the pouty smile
hangs on   her cross, a patch
of sky for a halo.   She says, See?

Violetta e Cristina

See how the bathers   stretch out   in the sun, sipping soft
drinks, nattering over   sandwiches, children   chasing shorebirds.
See how the Roma   girls trade   their trinkets, begging
as waves crush sand   castles and the bronzed   beachgoers bask.
Gabriel, in the crown   of a gopherwood,   surveys this scene.
A jet's silver wings   glint like shivs.   Young men, on a whim,
shove the gypsy girls   into the sea.   Laughter on the sand, screams
between the breakers. Legs   tangled in long   skirts, headscarves
tumbling in the surf. Why   does no one   seem upset by these
two faces covered   with bright beach   towels, blue feet
poking out, cold   in the sun? The ones   in uniform come and zip
them into vinyl bags,   carry them   past those lunching
or reclined still   on loungers   in the sand. Gabriel
lifts his horn.   See how   the bathers stretch out
in the sun, sipping soft   drinks, children   chasing shorebirds.

Them Which Were Vexed

Thirty-three stories   above these
city streets, in light   armor on a ledge,
hand on the hilt of a half   scabbarded sword,
he watches the one who   watches, waiting
for a sign. Tiny pedestrians   shuffle along
crosswalks below, cabs   idle at traffic
signals, lit windows   ascend into
the night. No one   seems to notice
the winged figure on the ledge   or the eye
that fills the open window   beside him,
as if it were gaping   through a peepshow
slot. Everything   appears black
and white to the watcher, the pedestrians,   the idling
cabs, the cement and steel   buildings. Only
a few witnesses huddled   together in a corner,
long beards spilling   over brightly
colored robes, cower   and swoon. One
tries to comfort another,   arm up
as if shielding his face   from the sun, as if
warding off a blow.   The eldest among
them, hands crossed   over his heart,
suppliant, lifts his   head to meet
the watcher's gaze. The eye   does not blink.

Lima South

The Filipino   with the pockmarked   face
said ten each,   hopped in the back   of the Ford
Econoline,   went to town,   a quick
sixty bucks,   dropped her at the corner,   Market
and High, blue   neon spelled *Clu*   *Utopia*
(the *b* was burned   out), parked   across
the street at Fidelity   (I shit you not)   Lumber,
the club was thick   with big black   cats
slamming back   Jack and Colt   45s,
a skinny skank   in a leopard leotard   spun
on her barstool,   said, Well looky   here,
crackers up   past they bedtime.   "Cold
Sweat" skipped   twice, crackled   on the juke.

Clot

She could sing silverfish   from the ceiling, clean skunk
guts out the tub   (damned dog), hurdle
the far fence   full canter, pick off
pigeons shitfaced   from fifty yards. When she
sashayed   through the stable, those raw hide
chaps hitched   up her hips made
me ponder the blood   squirming hogtied in my lap.

Backcountry

When the sun was not yet   half an hour high,
the bitterns rose croaking   from the reeds and circled the camp —
once, twice — before falling   on them in their slumber.
The couple flailed and kicked   at the soft, striped bodies.
The bitterns plucked and snipped.   Four vitreous marbles —
two blue, two brown — rolled   in the dust. The birds tussled,
sliding them down their long   gullets. There were cries and there
were whimpers. It was over   nearly before it had begun.
The night's embers smoldered   in the pit. And the bitterns lifted
one by one, flapping   lazily back to the stark
secrecy of the marsh. He called   out for her. They stumbled
over the tangled bedrolls,   feeling their way toward
the other's voice. The moon   waxes and the moon wanes.
They argue over the count   of days. What does it matter,
she says. They share the last   apple, each trying
to take smaller bites   than the other. Each day
they stay wrapped in their bedrolls   a little longer. They hold
one another until all   that's left is the holding. The bright
leaves finally let go,   covering them like a patchwork
quilt. The frost blackens   and bites. The bitterns raise
their bills skyward, necks   swaying, as if they are nothing
but reeds in the wind, as if   spellbound by some unsung hymn.

Still Life

When the grackles   disappeared   in the dune grass,
when the dune grass   swayed   in the seawind,
when the seawind   parted   the cottage drapes,
I saw you   sleeping   with your back towards the sea.

The seawind   lifted   a few strands, and,
in half sleep, you   tucked   them behind an ear.

Then the seawind   let   the drapes drop,
the dune grass   grew   still,
the grackles   rose   in a great flock,
and you   were   gone.

D

Am I   allowed to tell you now
how my face   flushed when you'd finished, how
the bile   burned in the back of my throat
maybe like   my sperm scalded yours
and how,   when you tried to kiss
me after and I   turned away, it wasn't
you, no,   it wasn't you?
Thirty   years gone, the shame
lingers.   You're still eighteen.
Forever   eighteen. We
were only   friends among friends, cruising
through the corn   haze of summer. I
don't know   why, but I
could barely   look at you after. Winter
came.   A patch of black ice,
an immovable   maple. You, forever
eighteen.   That girl, she wasn't, no,
it wasn't   you, just wax under that casket spray.

Chokecherry

When you return   to Tierra del Fuego,   my transmigratory
plover, scratch   a shallow depression   into the tundra,
and nest there still   as a sacred carving.   This voice
will call no more   for you, this bill   no longer
preen the down   warming your soft   throat. But, yes,
we'll always have   the small dark fruit we   gathered to fatten on.

Lucinda's Hands

Hot bituminous   bones, all   afternoon
I've been holding   them,   coveting
even this   kind of rectitude —   kerosene
ablutions   thinning the blue   layers
of lead   paint, my Shaker   chest
stripped   to bare   grain.

All afternoon,   I've kept   these
blood lilies   caged, their ruby   cubed
throats   poised like   Venus
flytraps — compound   eyes, exo-   skeleton
shucked   in the milky   spittle
that bubbles   round my   thorax.

If I   unfasten your   hands
from mine,   Lucinda, our   fingers
dried piles of pine   needles, will   you
rub your wrists   together like two   dead
sticks? Will you   breathe a little   light
into this   bonfire begging to   ignite?
Won't you   blow away   the dark
ash   that surrounds   us?

Wanted:

Ah, man, gimme   a coupla charms,
one purple, one   gold, of finches,
maybe a discrete murder   of crows yapping
at God knows what,   and stars tumbling,
the wind, the wind tripping   over the cedars
wrapped in shawls of snow,   this fire
and this dog, the promise   of June lilacs
and roses yet to bloom,   hell, I'd
even be glad (well   not quite)
for signs of a weed or two,   raccoons in the garbage,
the kid next door   playing spoons
out of tune, if   that's possible.
No cartoons   on the tube. I
guess there's nothing   left but
to sit and wait, for you,   for you.

October Last, Sally

Cover the cradle and close   the door,
let another   hour   slide by; the wind
takes the pretty   leaves from the trees
past these   panes of echoed sky.

Cover the cradle   and close   the door,
the sun will not   comply;   it scalds
and proves   their pampered   lies. No
matter. They   will deny,   deny. Why?

Cover   the cradle   and close the door,
help him   straighten his   tie; the dust
waits, open   the gate,   it's time to say
goodbye,   goodbye,   say goodbye.

Depth Charge

I am your injured sun,   listing a little
to port, opening fire   in a slow explosion
of grace. It is a threshold   beheld with wonder,
the veil lifted from the mouth   of a Persian girl,
purple tulips floating   in a bowl of milk.
Shall I establish this   forsaken beachhead?
Send in my mute   militia? I am
league eaten by the seas,   yet I rise, I rise
despite your bitter sabotage.   The cormorants,
those black rogues, hang   their wings in the seawind
to dry. The thick waves   advance with their nightsticks . . .

Positive Crankshaft Ventilation

It winnows away   the heat, and when   I wake,
not believing   in the advantages of friction   anymore,
or that all   those superbly   lubed parts,
moving as they do,   could generate   any meaning,
what then?

I move   slowly, carefully,   to the cupboard,
blow the dust   from the bottom   of a cup,
fill it   with last night's   coffee, add some
ice, and with my   first sip,   question
my motives.   Meanwhile,   having come
into the kitchen,   the   beautiful one
who flicks   her hair turns   towards me
with outstretched arms.

It's raining,   again, and   I can't
remember if   the car windows   are up.
She's smearing   orange   marmalade
onto her   biscuit, licking   her fingers
over the cutting   board, steam   rising
from my cup.   The rain   pummels
everything, blameless.

Nebuchadnezzar's Confession to Prometheus

When   those
towers   fell,
my   friend,
I   nearly
plucked   out
my   one
dumb   tongue
to   keep
from   song.

Lower Reserve

The son sits   at the father's right   hand
in Section 3,   Row Q,   Seats
11 and 12.   The home team   is up
one to nothing,   bottom of the 5th,   two
outs, runners   at the corners. The son   sips
a beer. He   has come straight   from work,
still in wingtips   and tie. He   would like
to talk with the father,   but only banalities   about
the ballgame and the long   stretch of fine   weather
pass between   them. He drinks. The father   comments
on the last pitch,   a nasty splitter   that jammed
their best hitter.   Foul ball   down
the left field   line. Strike   two.
The son wishes   the father would tell   him a few
things, things   about the weight   of work
and the trick of sacrifice   and maybe about   this
loneliness that she   and the kids can't seem   to touch.
The father signals   to the hotdog vendor,   passes
the money down   the row, tears   at the plastic
packet of mustard   with his teeth. Strike   three.
The visitors have stranded   two, inning   over.
The father finishes   the last bite,   wipes
the corner of his mouth   with a paper napkin,   drops
it at his feet.   He would like   to tell
the son that he misses   his boy, that he misses   his wife,
that the house plants   wither without   her.

The batter stands   in. First pitch   swinging.
If it stays fair,   it's a homerun.   They
are on their feet,   the ball arcing   out
of the lights into the seats.   The father and son   fight
for the ball, each frantic   to claim the keepsake   for the other.

Goodbye Is a BB Ricochets in Your Eye

reb

I poke around   his shack, plywood floors
rotted through,   bat shit on the workbench,
carpet of wood   shavings black with mold.
Too many   rusted cans of stain
stacked, unstacked,   lids lost, spirits
evaporated,   leaving behind petrified
dyes — cherry,   walnut, mahogany, oak.
A table leg   still locked in the lathe,
buttress tight   in the vice. A bird calls
in the fire bush   out back. No panes
left in these   windows, only broken
webs with their spun   husks of dead. You
better come on in,   she says, there's been a change.

The Lineman

Already power   lines sizzle   on someone's lawn,
lightning blares   in the trees, the blind   snaps

against the screen   as I count   the night miles
till thunder,   seconds between   bolts like you

taught me   on the porchswing   when I was scared.
Storms cuffed   their chill   off your buck

naked back, torrents   stinking of river,   transformers
sputtering angelic   white sparks   as you'd roar

off to fix   the darkness   in your yellow bucket
truck, salvaging   our town's light,   restringing

the broken lines   dangling so   dangerously near.
You let me go   with you once,   strobes spinning

through the fists   of rain. You spat   a *Lucky*'s
loose tobacco   from your lips,   two-way static

filling the cab.   With the knell   of your toolbelt
slung low,   in that thunderstruck   turbulence, you

tried to prove   something, rising   through the squalls
to the crossarms   heavy with blue   glass insulators.

I followed you   up those creosote   soaked poles,
splicing lines   of my own, feeling   the same scorch

on my skin, that cold   front refusing   to blow over.

The Final Syllable

This morning   I spooked,
or rather,   was spooked
by, a spruce   grouse that
nestled between   the geraniums
on the front porch.   I'd just
finished my first   cup of coffee
and had gone to fetch   the paper at the end
of the driveway.   At first I
thought it   was the neighbor's
cat, but then   it flit
into the hedgerow   and hunkered
down in the shadows.   I took
a slow step   to get a better
look. It   was a hen. She
bobbed her head   and caught my
eye through the green   needles. I
moved closer.   She paused
in her pretty feathers,   then flushed,
an exclamation   mark, and
was gone. Such   feral thoughts,
beyond all   explanation.

Ain't No Sense to Make of It
Lest You Call It What It Is

Them rainbows   was rising. Scooter matched
the hatch, tied on   an elkhair, arced his line
upstream,   riffles feeding the pool.
Around the bend,   something crested the creek,
maybe a buck.   He flicked the tip of the rod
skyward, set   the hook, he don't miss much.
He knows how they think.   He knows when to let
them dive deep,   when to tire them out
in the current. The water   carried on towards
the river that falls   to another that falls to the sea.
Them rainbows   was rising. I snagged
my line in the switches.   Scooter sang "Willow
Weep for Me,"   rainbows rising, rising
all around   us, waist deep in the kill.

To My Blue-Changed Opinion

We spit   between the splintered
trestle ties, hoping   carp would rise.
To the west some clouds   stacked into silos.
Willy hopped a rail,   arms stretched
out like a turkey vulture   circling the blue
sugar bowl of the sky   or Christ
hung out on his cross   to dry. It
was a long way down,   the mute brown
water restless in its bed.   The wind blew
out the sun. Willy   teetered, soft-
shoed on steel. In these   parts, they
say the worst storms   come on
sounding like freight   trains. C'mon,
we'd better get   to the other side.

Houses Hushed, Holy

Under the eaves   wasps mold   flutes
of mud, gray   papery prayers   against
the weather. Winds   unwind themselves,   tangle
in trees, tangle   in the loose reeds   of her
hair. She digs   among the young   turnips,
tethers snowpeas   to the trellis. Wasps   gather
the turned earth   in their intricate mouths.   She
knows which plants   to tear from the ground,   which
to water and feed,   which to watch over   and wait.
Only now   and again, when a bird   calls
or when she thinks   she hears the telephone   ring,
does she look up   from the furrows. Wasps   glide
between the eaves   and her garden, brittle   wings
glittering, blue   bodies throbbing   in the mud.
She looks   back at the dark   rows.
Soon she'll spray   the wasps away   with a hose.

Every Day Is Arbitrary

Scooter points   the 'cuda up   Mudsock,
pops the clutch,   tires spin   blue
smoke, fishtail,   tach running   red.
Quick shift,   the blond cows   blur.
Speedometer tips   the century mark.   I
lean out,   wind up,   the longneck
decapitates a mailbox.   Downshift, lurch   forward,
cut hard   right onto Infirmary,   headers
humming. The eight   track clicks   midsong.
We both   knew what time   it was.
Time enough   and time too   little.
Then time   and when time.   You
swapped the 'cuda   for a punch buggy,   ping-
pinged off   to school, a baggie   of grass
under the seat,   Wittgenstein, Niebuhr,   Blake,
that girl   from Tipp City,   Spain
in the spring. You   made partner at thirty,   play
tennis at two   every Thursday.   I saw
your picture in the paper,   it was Wednesday or maybe   Saturday.
I drove out   past the gravel   pits,
our unwavering grain   elevator slipping from   my rearview.

Hypotheses

If   it is true   that the feather
evolved   for flight   from its original
purpose   of sustaining   warmth,
then   the lunging   of wolves
delivers   the annunciations   of those
who   wait in   the corn —

If   it is true   that the darkness
lingers   even when   the light reigns,
then   the famished   squadrons
seaward   capsized   swoon
under   the wailing   of stars —

If   it is true   that Nero
gazed   at his   gladiators
through   an emerald   eyepiece,
then   the irrepressible   ribcage
of   the bow-and-   arrow boy
rings   with haunted   doves —

And   you and I will   drink milk
then   after the rain   at the mill
with   tears of laughter,   if
it   is   true.

Where All That Walks Wild Is

Because I abandoned   boots below
timberline, I   rest on a ridge
rubbing these raw   feet, laboring
for breath among lichen   laced boulders,
some kind of sparrow   stirs in the scrub,
flits near, unafraid,   were I so
fortunate myself, middle   aged man
in the midst of distant   mountains,
pondering, no   Moses moment
comes, this walking   stick no
holy staff, just   a stick I
stumbled on, or over,   the coyotes keep
yodeling with those damned   yucca tongues.

First Adultery

Afterwards,   they lay listening   to the bullfrogs,
the low   moan of an owl   near the edge of the field,
leaves   of corn whispering   secrets among the furrows.
The canal   split open   over the broken
lock,   then sealed itself   again. What
the water   could not consume —   logs, a crippled
plough,   the moon — it would harrow,   unhappy with its fate
between   the narrow banks   where mules and barge
masters   trod. Somewhere   across these fields,
a man   scours a shotgun,   a rabbit screams,
the farm   dogs prick up   their ears. Somewhere
across   this field, a wife   sleeps on a porchswing,
lightning   bugs beckon,   a radio evangelist
urges   us not to yield.   What they have,
they   have borrowed. Yellow   flowers sown
in the bones   of the water like   new marrow.

Stutter

He wore a stained   godfather,
stuck singed   cock feathers in the silk
band, punched tin   cross strung
on a bootlace   around his neck. Deep
in the woods, he told   fortunes by the feet
of box turtles,   slept in the crook of an elder
tree at noon. Deer   ticks swelled
under our shirts.   Leaves ticked in the dry
wind. When he mouthed   that old harpoon
and sang   "In the Garden," even
the shadblow seemed   ashamed. Night
jars whistled.   June bugs woke
the moon. We followed   the mink runs
along the river,   caught some girls
skinny dipping in our hole   by the trestle.
He dropped   to his knees in the mud and placed
his hat on the water.   Wasn't a single
one of us   didn't bow our heads
as he bit down   on that clumsy
tongue till the blood   gushed like a psalm.

Obedience

A man stands over   a dog, pointing .
down at its raised muzzle.   The dog sits,
wagging. The man keeps   pointing. He is
explaining something to the dog.   The dog sits,
wagging. The man cocks   his head slightly
for emphasis. He is still   pointing. His lips
move, but the wind rips   his words away,
fragments of syllable and sound,   pieces of a name
perhaps, perhaps a shred   of command. He
holsters his finger, and they   resume their walk
down the lane. The dog   keeps lifting
its head, checking in,   wagging whenever
the man speaks. The man   stops again,
gives the dog a pat.   The dog sits,
wagging. The dog sits.   Wagging.

Maybe Stink

Then Christ is gonna   come and wire   shut
the jaws of the tulips,   he says, and the   God
of Abraham's gonna   fill our Bolivian   lamps
with salt from   the desert. Stink says   stuff
like this sometimes.   He seems serious   enough,
but it can be   tough to tell with   Stink.
Widows will pin   black lace into their   hair,
caesuras disguised   as prayers hidden in their   blouses.
Stink, man,   do you even know   what
a caesura is?   Don't matter none, says   he,
I just say   what comes into my   head.
But what   does it mean? Beats all   hell
outta me, I   just like singing them   words.